LOVEPLAY
A Conversation in Rhyme

LOVEPLAY
A Conversation in Rhyme

Joe Fromstein & Linda Stitt

2004
White Knight Publications
Toronto, Canada

Published in 2004 by White Knight Publications,
a division of Bill Belfontaine Ltd.
Suite 103, One Benvenuto Place
Toronto Ontario Canada M4V 2L1
T. 416-925-6458 F. 416-925-4165
e-mail: whitekn@istar.ca

National Library of Canada Cataloguing in Publication

Fromstein, Joe, 1918-

Loveplay : a conversation in rhyme / Joe Fromstein and Linda Stitt.

ISBN 0-9734186-7-2

1. Man-woman relationships—Poetry.

I. Stitt, Linda, 1932- II. Title.

PS8611.R65L68 2004   C811'.6   C2004-903268-2

Editor: Sharon Singer
Cover Art: Rolland Proulx
Interior design by Karen Petherick,
Intuitive Design International Ltd.

Printed and Bound in Canada

Dedication

by Joe Fromstein

This book is dedicated to the cherished memory of my wonderful wife Bertha. She constantly encouraged me and was an honest critic whose candid input seldom failed to improve my poems. She was my mate, my lover, my best friend, my inspiration and ever the prime source of my happiness until her death due to cancer seven years ago. I will miss her and love her always.

She was a beautiful woman, an amazing artist whose paintings were eloquent and imaginative. She was constantly studying and experimenting with unusual techniques. Her intellect was as keen as her capacity to love, and she has left behind a legacy of integrity, creativity and loyalty which continues to exert a beneficent and enduring effect on all who knew her well.

Contents

Contents

Contents

Acknowledgements

by Joe Fromstein

Sharon Singer, a fellow poet, conceived the book's title and was invaluable as an editorial consultant in stimulating the process of preparing this book. She not only did a terrific editing job, she also guided me through every stage involved in the process, and was most responsible for getting everything ready for the publisher. I will always be grateful for her unstinting and intelligent help in bringing this book to fruition.

My daughter Rhonda did all the typing. She tackled the numerous revisions with cheerfulness and enthusiasm, and performed with alacrity. Her mastery of the computer was critical, and I am obliged to her for having been constantly on call. Thanks a lot, Rhonda.

Rolland Proulx was imaginative in his concept and design of the elegant book cover and he did the photographic work. I was fortunate to be able to benefit from his excellent suggestions, inspired intuition and continuous encouragement.

My children, Mike and wife Amy, my children Stevie and Rhonda, my grandchildren Joel, Daniel, David and Maya, and my dear friend Joyce Lieberman were constant sources of support.

I want to thank Steven Michael Berzensky for his editorial consultation and advice, often on long distance from Saskatchewan, but always unfailing in its judgment and vision.

I appreciate the enthusiastic responses to the book by experts in humor like Mike Bullard, Tom Arnold, Brett Butler, Mark Breslin, and others.

My publisher, Bill Belfontaine, was crucial in bringing this book into being. I am grateful to him for his suggestions and guidance. It would be difficult to exaggerate the significance of his faith in the merit of the contents. Thanks, Bill.

And finally, I am filled with admiration for Linda. But for her witty, thought-provoking poems mine would never have been written. Her considerate cooperation in giving me permission to use them made everything possible. I will always be aware that this book exists mainly because of her.

Introduction

by Joe Fromstein

This collaborative book was born in an accidental way. My niece, Sharon Singer, a published poet, invited me along several years ago to a reading by Linda Stitt which she was sure I would find delightful. Sharon's optimism turned out to be an understatement: Linda was a captivating performer. Her work radiates charm, intellect and humor.

During the reading of one of her poems I thought of a line that would fit perfectly into the middle of it. So, when she finished, I caught her eye and said: "Would you please deliver that poem again. You left out a line." She must have been astonished at this strange interjection. But she was a good sport, and curious too, so she agreed. At the place for my insert I held up my hand and recited my line. It did fit right in, with the same rhyme and meter as Linda's, and we all had a good laugh.

Linda was so impressed by my enthusiastic reaction to her work that she gave me a copy of her book. Among its many witty, entertaining poems was a funny one called "The First Time," about an imagined sexual adventure. It immediately summoned a poetic reply, which I called "The Last Time." The next time I attended Linda's reading I showed it to her. She liked it enough to ask me to read it to her audience as a response to hers, and we were a hit!

Well, that started the ball rolling. I acquired all of Linda's published books and perused them in search of other poems that stimulated my imagination. After a while I had quite a few and we even read together in bookstores like Chapters and Nicholas Hoare's in Toronto, and in other venues like restaurants and at private affairs. It was great fun and we became good friends.

In this fortuitous way there came into being a collection embracing Linda's poems, seen on the left, and my responses to them, on the right, like an unspoken conversation. On a rare occasion I got the first word in and we reversed the order.

My son Steve urged me to put my poems into some kind of order, like, for instance, a book. When I asked him who would ever be interested in reading it he at once replied "me!" Thus, assured of a readership of at least one, I paired them with Linda's poems, which had inspired them, and ended up with this creation.

Encouragement for this project came from an enthusiastic array of family and friends. If they were sincere I shall be forever grateful. If it turns out they were just kidding, I'll make sure they're each stuck with a copy of this book, and it will serve them right.

For Sol

Read me your poetry,
listen to mine,
pour me a truth like an
excellent wine.
Nothing but soberness
have we to lose,
sharing a toast to our
mutual muse.

"Help!"

Reading is easy
but writing's an art,
bound to intimidate
right from the start.
I shall attempt it,
and that is my oath,
if your inspiration's
enough for us both.

The First Time

Let's keep it cool and let's keep it light,
come on baby, I don't have all night,
if we're gonna do it, let's do it right
the first time.

I can't recall just how or who
but I think he was probably a lot like you
and it must have been fine or I'd have been through
the first time.

And it got to be my favourite pastime
but I don't even remember the last time,
so let's make sure this is real high-class time
the first time.

At this juncture, one expects I'm
not gonna get a lot of sex time,
so don't leave anything to next time
the first time.

Hot and heavy may come later
in the linen closet or the elevator,
but let's take a good time and make it greater
the first time.

The Last Time

Once thought I'd never get my fill,
and probably I never will,
but still, it felt like army drill
the last time.

Two bodies, clothes on none of them,
lying, just for the fun of them,
and I think that mine was one of them,
the last time.

The episode won't bring me fame,
I didn't even know the dame
and yet, I wish I'd got her name,
the last time.

Her age escaped my close attention.
I don't know why she had to mention
she was applying for her pension
the last time.

It wasn't very hard to take.
But I thought it might be a mistake
when I found I could hardly stay awake
the last time.

These days it brings, to some degree,
exhaustion more than ecstasy,
and I fear each time that it may be
the last time.

Small Request

If, as you say, you love me well,
give me an abalone shell,
a pebble with a pearly lustre,
a little star from the Virgo cluster.
Find me a peacock's fallen feather,
an April day of perfect weather,
a drop of resin from a spruce,
a sip of pomegranate juice.
Give me a flake of crystal snow,
a lake where water lilies grow,
a whisper of cloud hung out to dry
in a cerulean space of sky,
an autumn moon in a yellow wedge,
a sunset over the ocean's edge.
A gift of one of these would show
how much you care, how well you know.

But, if you love me as you say,
give me a moment of your day,
find a place where we can be
alone together, you and me.
Then, if it's not too much to ask,
show me what's underneath the mask.

Believe Me

It's not a mask! It's really me.
Perhaps it's time for me to see
a plastic surgeon. I would dare
if it were paid by Medicare.
Enough of that. Now to the task
of bringing everything you ask.
If shells and pebbles, resins, juice,
the antlers of an angry moose,
the teeth of a Komodo dragon,
the canvas from a covered wagon –
could these win your elusive favour,
the greatest danger I would savour.
I'd face a lion in a rage
if it were locked within its cage.
I'd wrap a beam of golden light
in rainbows just for your delight.
The scent of every fragrant flower –
this I would bring you every hour,
rare gems from some exotic shore
to grace the one that I adore.

All this should show my dedication,
my relentless fascination.
But, if you still want some "outer-space" gift,
I might agree to have a face-lift.

The Poet As Petitioner
or
The Reading As Pleading

Hear me as a lover hears.
Tender me that sweet attention
touching in those secret places
far too sensitive to mention.
Lend me more than just your ears;
hear me as a lover hears.
Focus every sense on me
in rapt intensity and be
attentive to my shameless plea
to hear with more than just your ears.
Listen to me with your heart;
let this sorry rush outpouring
fall upon a hush adoring.
I acknowledge, at the start,
my shortcomings and my fears
of critical, unloving ears.
Literate, discriminating
you may be. But even so,
for a kind, accommodating
moment, let detachment go
and hear me with a lover's ears.
I'm doing this for love, you know.

I Like You Too

This great suggestion you have made
(if I can trust my hearing aid)
will head a formidable list
of tempting things I can't resist.
Though the specific body part
responding may not be my heart,
if I don't like all lovers hear,
I can pretend to be sincere.
Your reference to secret places
makes me yearn for your embraces,
yet no matter how I try
I can't get over being shy.
Those areas so highly prized
have me completely paralysed.
It's not as if I fear or mind them
and I'm pretty sure that I can find them,
but, to satisfy your thirst,
I think that you should touch me first.
Then I shall let detachment go;
I'm doing this for lust, you know.

First Date

I am so flexible, so undemanding,
witty and wonderful, truly outstanding,
fey and ethereal, such a wee elf,
thoroughly, heartily sick of myself.

He's such a gentleman, so debonair,
charming, intelligent, devil-may-care,
dripping with chivalry, classy and clever –
God, must this evening continue forever.

Same Date

She may be as charming and sweet as she seems
but she isn't the answer to all of my dreams.
She laughs at my jokes, whether blatant or indirect,
which shows an advanced and astute intellect.

But we've nothing in common, no fanciful
    flight share,
so this is beginning to feel like a nightmare,
and though the word "blind" is assigned to this
    date
I can <u>see</u> that we will not be staying up late.

She acts quite compatible most of the time;
she looks pretty good, though she's not in her
    prime;
but, though she may not be the beauty I've sought,
at least I can tell that she likes <u>me</u> a lot.

Reservations Not Required

I had a long discussion with you, in my head,
explaining how I hoped you hadn't been misled
but that too many friendships had been lost in bed
to passion, when I craved companionship instead.
I told you that I didn't want a casual affair
and one-to-one relationships, these days, are pretty rare.
My expectations, I allowed, are seldom realistic
and I didn't need that proven by another sad statistic.
I said I feared commitment was, for me, too great a task;
– but suddenly I realized I hadn't heard you ask.

Taking A Chance

Okay, I'm asking! But it's true
I've had some reservations too.
I feared just caring for a bit meant
it might lead to a commitment.
Freedom has been my greatest treasure,
but there are other kinds of pleasure.
So, to myself, my own advice is,
be prepared for sacrifices.
The rewards will be divine,
days of joy be yours and mine,
affection that cements and binds,
and lasts – until we change our minds.

Good Night

Please, my friend, try not to think me
inhospitable or rude,
but when midnight comes, it finds me
longing for my solitude.
This is where I love and leave you,
I've commitments I must keep,
now's the time I lay me down
along the starry banks of sleep.
Lay me down and spread my net
across the river of my dreams,
sift them through until I find one
so substantial that is seems
strong enough that I may mount it,
trust it, let it carry me,
past the rapids of distraction
with the current, to the sea.
There within the ocean's vapours
dream and dreamer are the same.
When I waken in the morning,
I'll recall my daylight name.
But at night I mix my essence
with my sustenance, and so
I must beg your leave to leave you,
it is late and I must go.

Wait For Me

Stay. Perhaps the day is ending
but the morning's scarce begun,
and the message you are sending
is misleading if you run.
I'm enthused, alert, inspired,
and I wish you felt that way.
I am neither bored nor tired –
perhaps because I've slept all day.
So, if you're more than just a friend,
and that, to me, is how it seems,
why can't I, with the evening's end,
go travelling with you in your dreams?
Both of us then could soar aloft
as though suspended from a star,
where gods of old ambrosia quaffed
while viewing mortals from afar.
Stay with me a little longer,
wait awhile for your repose,
watching as our bonds grow stronger
and our lovely friendship grows.

That's Life

I've met many a woman, forsooth,
since the days of my innocent youth,
and I've always succeeded
as much as I needed
except when I've told them the truth.

Ex-oneration
or
Nameless, Blameless And Out To Launch

Don't think of yourself as a loser,
a failure, a promise unkept.
Consider that you are the springboard from which
a lot of good women have leapt.

Worry Time

My life is full of problems
and worries that I nurse.
My only expectations are
that they'll be getting worse.
The fates are acting up,
and have me feeling down;
if things don't soon improve
I'm hiding, out of town.
Then worries will be behind me,
at least, until they find me.

No Trouble At All

No need to flee from trouble,
just look it in the eye
and tell yourself
that you can see
its bright side, if you try,
and a cloud on the horizon
simply means that, by and by,
there's every chance
that there will be
a rainbow in your sky.

For Michael – In Retrospect

No wonder I happened to think about you,
I'm wearing your hand-me-down hose.
In case you've forgotten,
they're dingy old cotton
with holes in the heels and the toes.
I found you adrift without compass or oars,
I saw that you needed direction;
I loaned you some socks
and the key to my locks
and I gave you my tender affection.
I offered you all that a woman can give –
I guess that I wasn't too smart –
to persuade you to stay
but you wandered away
with my best woolen socks and my heart.
You bore me no malice, I wish you no ill,
I would not, if I could, turn my clocks back.
My heart has not faltered,
my locks have been altered,
but some day I would like my socks back.

Some Day, Maybe

My own mother once tried to disown me.
I'm reviled by most people who've known me.
But you cause me more pain when you choose to complain
about some of the clothing you loaned me.

Now, it's true that you treated me well,
and we had a few laughs for a spell,
but I always depart from affairs of the heart
when the heaven starts feeling like hell.

So I hope you'll stop shedding a tear
for those socks that I've had for a year,
and my only excuse, since they're not put to use,
is, they make such a fine souvenir.

I was never inclined to romance,
and our meeting was purely by chance,
so forget those old socks that were heavy as rocks
and feel lucky it wasn't your pants.

Summer Day

A froth of clouds across the blue,
a quality of air,
a breeze that moves my silk about
and lifts my sun-soaked hair,
a heat that bakes my winter bones,
flowers to drench my eye,
a lovely, lazy lassitude,
– this is my July.

My Summer Day

Some infra rays to scorch my skin,
with *burn* the prime sensation,
enveloping my body in
a bath of perspiration,
while air that's harder to inhale,
and worse than I remember,
has got me longing for the gale
that greets me in December.

or

My July

The rain attacking like a flood
to wash away my flowers,
mosquitoes sucking on my blood,
enjoying it for hours,
a sun that's glowing in the sky,
when clouds will let it in,
aware the only reason why
is just to dry my skin;
this is my July.
Besides, it is beyond dispute
that I look like hell in a bathing suit.

How I hate July!

Lyrics For A Country('s) Song

I have learned, to my grief,
that your promises are big
but the chances of your keeping them are small.
If you're not gonna do
what you say you're gonna do,
why bother saying it at all?

If I counted on you
I'd be right up the creek,
up the stream, up the brook, up the river.
Why take the trouble
to take my order
if you know you're not gonna deliver?

Maybe you're convinced
that you're doing me a favour,
saying what you think I want to hear.
But I warn you,
if you can't stop bending the truth,
you'd better stop bending my ear.

Is that clear?

Telling me lies
isn't cool, isn't wise;
take a lesson, take a hint, take a note,
if you don't get the message
get ready to get dumped,
'cause you're not gonna get my vote.

Lying To Linda

My talks of vacations
to tempting locations –
I know how thrilled you always are to hear them,
but it's more like invention
than genuine intention:
we both know that you'll never end up near them.

I find it nerve-wracking
just thinking of packing,
afraid I might forget my medication.
I start to unravel
just thinking of travel:
my only joy is in anticipation.

The weight of each bag,
the fear of jet lag,
are worrisome as flies stuck in the ointment.
So when I'm staying put,
or just traveling by foot,
that's my way of avoiding disappointment.

So grant me protection
from loss of your affection,
if we should part, forever I would rue it.
Do find it in you
to let me continue:
I'd hate to think I had a chance, and blew it.

My plans make sense,
there's little expense,
imaginary trips can be sublime.
Our health's not tested,
we're always rested,
and – I think I really meant it at the time.

Litterally Speaking

We're going to need separate quarters, to keep
our relationship smooth and serene,
for you are obsessively messy, my sweet,
and I am compulsively clean.

Although I'm delighted to be where you are
and treasure the moments we share,
the permanent litter that lies in your wake
is more than a body can bear.

For us to attempt to encourage our love
in a common abode would be utter
disaster, since you can't survive where it's neat
and I cannot live amidst clutter.

Plea Of A Slop

My possessions, it's true, are all over the place,
but I can't figure out why you mind them,
for there's method involved in the chaos you face
and wherever things are, I can find them.

When you make up my bed without wrinkle or crease,
which I know never happened before,
I'm so anxious to cause your complaining to cease
that I'm willing to sleep on the floor.

So give me a chance to reform, once again,
and retain all the joys I have known,
for you're one of a kind, you are more than a ten,
and – I'd hate to be sleeping alone.

Falling Flat

We made some sparks and we made some light,
we made some noises in the night,
we made a merry time alright,
but we never made music.

We made a picture, chic and smart,
of excellence in head and heart.
We made ourselves a work of art,
but we never made music.

We made an effort, more or less,
the best that we could do, I guess.
We made a moderate success,
but we never made music.

We made a modicum of hay,
we made our uncommitted way.
We made some moves that made our day,
but we never made music.

We made no effort to deceive,
we tucked no ace up any sleeve.
We made a game of make believe,
but we never made music.

We made it through from dusk to dawn,
but your memory is almost gone
for only melody lingers on
and we never did make music.

Find A Musician

I thought that we might get along
and sing each other love's sweet song;
it's not the first time I was wrong,
so we couldn't make music.

In days gone by, when Zeus was king
and was inclined to have a fling,
no harp or piano did *he* bring,
but, *he* didn't need music.

Beethoven's famous far and near
for music that he couldn't hear,
yet lost the one that he held dear,
even though he made music.

Byron charmed his lady fair
with poetry beyond compare,
I read this, but I wasn't there,
so maybe he made music.

Shakespeare, whom I love to quote,
many charming sonnets wrote –
but *he* couldn't read a note,
so why should *I* need music?

I thought that you were heaven sent,
that each was for the other meant,
but I couldn't play an instrument.

So spare me this polite harangue;
you couldn't stand it when I sang,
so, how could we make music?

Two-Night Stand

You left on a grey December evening
when the sun was a hundred years away.
I turned on all the heaters.
> I was too proud to ask you to stay,
> too insecure to think that you might want to.

Now, restless as the long night comes
and hungry, I curse myself
for having banqueted on crumbs
that only served to waken
slumbering appetite.
> Ah, well, never mind,
it shall sleep again, and I forgive
my meagre feast.
> But still, my friend, I find
a kernel of regret within your going.

My sorrow is for you, that you have wasted
ambrosia untouched upon your plate.
> There is so much of me you have not tasted.

I'm Getting Hungry

I've missed an opportunity sublime
because I wasn't hungry at the time.
But if I'm ever in the same position
I'll know you are a great source of nutrition.

I previously thought you were a female,
though sweet and charming, one I could replace
by turning to my ever present e-mail
to fetch a substitute from cyberspace.

I'm glad that you have banished my illusion.
It's more than gratitude you've made me feel.
From now on there will be no more confusion.
I'll simply look upon you as a meal.

Sing Me Your Love Song

Sing me your love song one last time,
your groans, your whispers and your sighs,
sing me a farewell lullaby, for I'm
about to close my eyes
and sleep for a thousand years.

And maybe, when the planet has revolved
one hundred decades round the sun,
the twists and turns of time shall have resolved
this icy labyrinth, which will not be dissolved
by the solution of my tears.

Wish me a dreamless sleep.
I do not want to tread again
where dreams have taken me.
And if your kiss,
ten centuries away,
can only echo this
frozen and hopeless now,
then do not waken me.

Stay Awake

That sleep to which you now refer
is many decades premature.
For if you hasten into slumber
years without end, and beyond number,
just as I was almost ready
to suggest that we go steady,
I'd feel obliged to go along,
and if I did, we'd both be wrong.
Avoid that long and weary climb
through all those centuries of time.
I fear the worst catastrophe –
that you may not remember me.
Since you're almost always wise
let's agree to compromise:
sleep a few days and dream of bliss
and I *will* wake you with a kiss.
Then, since with goddesses of old I rank you,
at least you should get up and say: "I thank you."

Time

Time is wealth and time is treasure.
Give me time for lazy leisure.
Give me time in waves and billows,
heaped on cushions, piled on pillows,
time extravagant, and lush.
Let me never have to rush.
Lavish on me hours luxurious
to indulge in being curious,
– time to explore, time to ignore
obligations that press where I'm already sore;
time I have no need to budget
so I never will begrudge it.
Give me time for sloth and sinful
torpor, by the pail and binful,
time in torrents and in showers,
floods of minutes, seas of hours;
time profuse and time galore
where there was no time before;
time to waste and time to wander,
aimless, blameless time to squander;
time unmortgaged and unpledged
to scrutinize the mind-gems dredged
from deepest memory, where they
have lain in careless disarray
awaiting due consideration.
Give me time for meditation,
where the benefits inherent
may not be at once apparent.
Investing so, I can depend
on an eternal dividend.
Tear my calendar to tatters.
Give me time for foolish matters,
time to lay a dream and hatch it.
Take my Timex and dispatch it.
Shred my schedule; kick my clock;
cancel all my dates. Unlock
me from agendas. Set me free.
I've served my time. Let time serve me.

It's About Time

I'm king of time and at your service.
Don't be shocked and don't be nervous;
I'm little known but fully booked,
though oft alone and overlooked.
You're the best poet in the west
so I am granting your request.
If you use well this priceless power
I will not charge you by the hour.
Just probe your avenues of time,
capture ideas and themes sublime,
bringing the essence of them home
as dazzling thought or deathless poem.
You may be curious as to why
the other gods who never die
are better known and highly prized –
it's just because they advertised!
They lobbied every kind of shrine
and bragged about their birth divine;
they made predictions, gave advice,
were often wrong and seldom nice.
And you may be a bit surprised
to learn that one was circumcised.
It happened when Apollo's son,
a surgeon out to have some fun,
sliced his patient's you-know-what up,
and was thenceforth called a cut-up.

I could go on and on and on
but the time I can spare is almost gone.
You know how precious it can be,
you don't spend as much as I'd like with me,
though the tales I could tell would make you as glad
as the ones that were told by Scheherazade.
But – if time is what this is all about,
I have to inform you – it just ran out.

Going To The Dogs

Age has turned my corners down
and lengthened all my bulges.
The dreadful truth my bangs disguise
my double chin divulges.
The bloom of youth has gone to seed,
the gilt is off the lily
and here I am in puppy love.
My goodness, I feel silly.

Ideal Partners

Deep wrinkles decorate my brow,
for absent hair I pine.
My teeth are linked by bridges now,
though all of them are mine.
Old age has me in its clutches,
joints are no longer supple,
soon I may be needing crutches –
we'll make a perfect couple!

Artichokes

How can I trust that your heart is pure,
your values valid,
while you sit there picking the artichokes
out of your salad.

Artichokes Rejected

I've always hated artichokes,
which I have never tried,
but I will eat most anything
that's resting by their side.
My heart is pure enough without them,
so let's hear nothing more about them.

Cold Comfort

When I'm flat on my back, looking up at the sky,
with a tear in my pants and a tear in my eye,
the last thing I need is for you to come by
and tell me it might have been worse.

When all my defences have seen fit to fail me
and worries and doubts and terrors assail me,
don't feel it your duty to heartily hail me
insisting it might have been worse.

When keen-edged injustice has cut to the quick
and the shit flung by fortune has started to stick,
don't offer, like some sanctimonious prick,
the theory it might have been worse.

When I'm in the clutches of doom and despair
over matters of health, or the heart, I don't care
to be comforted, soothed or consoled. Don't you dare,
as they're coming for me with the hearse,
to tell me it might have been worse.

Warm Comfort

When your house was destroyed and they broadcast the news
you were sure you had no more possessions to lose,
but I saw you still wearing your favourite shoes,
so I guess that it could have been worse.

Then you finally landed that guy with the beard
and were swept into rapture, but, just as I feared,
your best friend arrived and they both disappeared –
still, I'm sure that it could have been worse.

You were slicing your bread and a finger was cleft,
you were feeling discouraged and slightly bereft;
I reminded you then of the nine you had left
but your only response was to curse.

But every disaster, misfortune or blight
can divulge, if you seek it, a side that is bright:
it could always be worse, don't you see?
All those things might have happened to ME.

Satchel Ass

In trying to pose as a slut,
I just couldn't manage the strut.
I mastered the talk
but could not walk the walk.
I think it's the shape of my butt.

Count On Me

If the life of a slut is for you,
and I think you'd be good at it too,
if it's practice you need
I can help you succeed;
as a friend, it's the least I can do.

Conformity

Today I re-established hope,
I washed myself with scented soap,
I rouged my cheeks and shaved my shins
and did my tresses up in pins.
I splashed perfume behind my knees
and walked among the chimpanzees
and not a one of them could see
the monkey I had made of me.

Memory Stretch

I used to be a chimpanzee;
that was the story told to me
by one, a psychic by profession,
who specialized in retrogression.
And I remembered, from my trance,
a scene where some exotic dance
had been performed with charm and grace
by one with rouge upon her face
and perfume splashed behind her knees
that was so strong it made me sneeze.
I fell in love, conceived a plan
that helped transform me to a man ...
     I seek that vision everywhere
     to know the joy her presence gave,
     to tell her just how much I care –
     then get her to become my slave.

Thank You Not

Thank you for sparing the time
from your intellectual quest
to concern yourself
with my petty affairs.
I'm so gratified that
somebody like you
should busy himself
with my humble pursuits.
Not everyone cares.
I'm sure that my business will benefit
from your involvement
and your incisive analysis.
You're unspeakably kind
to have offered a piece of your mind
with your brain in the grip of paralysis.

It's Nice To Be Appreciated

Though you're jokingly acting so hateful
I am sure that deep down you are grateful,
and appreciate wisdom I'm sharing
because I'm so thoughtful and caring.
So please don't consider me errant,
but your flaws are so great and transparent
that a gentleman couldn't stand by
when his brilliant assistance was nigh.
So I hope you'll consider us friends
with no need for my making amends.
This would make me so happy that when
you need more advice,
then quick as a trice,
I'll try to be helpful again.

Softly, Softly

Poetry's a fragile gift,
in my estimation;
it may shatter on the blade
of ratiocination.
Intuition's gentle wand
brings it best to balance.
Discipline it lightly,
it's the tenderest of talents.

Growing Poetry

My poetry is plant life
that I water every day,
in hopes that there is nourishment
embedded in the clay.
But sometimes, when it's fully grown,
developed from the seed,
I find that all there is to show
is a huge, repulsive weed.

The Lineup

I think I see the pattern now,
I recognize the game I've played,
our parting leaves my love intact,
it might have faltered if you'd stayed.

I build a noble fantasy
but soon my pettiness, my fears,
my little insecurities
would bring it crashing round my ears.

And so it's easier for me
to let you go and bear the pain
than watch the slow erosion of
commitment I could not sustain.

Now I can put your picture up
with all the others on the shelf
and mourn a monumental loss
and never have to face myself.

End Of The Line

Your gallery of victims shows,
much more than portraits on a shelf,
it's possible, the more it grows,
the more you grow to love yourself.

Each escapade has been, till now,
an evanescent, fleeting thing.
Perhaps it's time to take a vow
instead of just another fling.

Forget the conquests you hold dear.
Let a new you put a sign up,
saying: "I've someone special here,
so no one else can join the lineup."

You'd trust a surgeon with his knife,
and welcome every fragile suture.
So why not trust *me* with your life;
you're only gambling with your future.

Understanding Angels

Angels, I am told,
do not impose themselves,
they come by invitation.
Ever present,
they do not intrude
or appear unbidden;
their ministrations
are ubiquitous,
but hidden.
Their constant visitation will rarely
    rise to consciousness
without some preparation,
some prayer or contemplation
or simple recognition
of realms beyond mundane preoccupation,
    dimensions of peace and healing
    and compassionate vibration.

Acknowledge angels;
accept with gratitude
the clear realization
that they are with us always,
helping, protecting, guiding,
leading us into love and liberation.

Open yourself to angels;
    beings of light,
    they bear illumination.

An Angel's Soliloquy

I am an angel.
Once, an exemplary, marvelous mortal,
beckoned beyond that invisible portal,
destined as though by some noble decree
to elevate people to be just like me.
Most humans progress at the pace of a snail;
my tasks become daunting, and sometimes I fail.
But I'm never discouraged, my head is unbowed,
because acting like humans just isn't allowed.
Yet I have some restrictions I think are unfair,
like not being able to show that I'm there.
I enter their minds when I'm sneaking behind them,
I search for the conscience but can't always find them.
My home's not some kind of vacation resort.
I wonder each night if they'll like my report.
Successes are filed while my failures are noted
and if there are many I don't get promoted.
I relish my work and I hate to complain
and I wouldn't prefer to be human again,
so whenever you sense some invisible guide
it may be that I'm silently there at your side
and I'd deem it a favor if you'd see the light
and decide for a change that you'll do what is right.

The Sophisticates

We nursed our illusion of love,
for its death was too tasteless to mention,
and cultured our mutual scorn
for suburban and civic convention.
We were two of the beautiful folk,
not the rabble that whistles and sniffs.
We were charming and witty and chic
and too civil for squabbles and tiffs.
We directed our barbs with aplomb
while carefully keeping our heads,
for if we had aimed at those we most loathed
we'd have torn one another to shreds.

Let's Get Along

I'm glad that your hatred's divulged,
your most candid of feelings indulged.
Though hypocrisy's battering
truth can be shattering
just like an artery bulged.

I'm not saying it isn't your fault,
but, like treasures you store in a vault,
the delights from "back when"
could be ours once again
if we stopped treating blisters with salt.

How Was It For You, Baby?

For me, it wasn't very much,
a rediscovering of touch,
electric tremors up my spine
and in the darkness, inner shine
of liquids luminous and warm;
a redesigning of my form
melting and reshaping to
accommodate itself to you.
Sinuous, sensuous skin to clasp
spasmodically, a moan, a gasp,
a sun gone nova, nothing new –
how was it, my beloved, for you?

Do You Want The Truth?

For me, I'm really still not sure,
in spite of your charms and your allure,
'cause I wonder if what you wish to share
pertains to the night when I was there.
For I wasn't exactly in your debt
while your eyes were glued to the T.V. set,
and you weren't on the road to undying fame
when you called me by someone else's name.
But still, if the truth must now be known,
it was better by far than being alone.
So when you run short of other men,
just call and we'll do it once again,
for I found more joy while you were there
than I ever had in a dentist's chair;
and I'm grateful, since you're so sweet and pure,
that I've caught no disease that has no cure.

Death Wish

Do not pollute my final breath
with whimpering and whining,
but say how sweet the lindens smell
and that the sun is shining.

Sing me a song of thankfulness
and, if you can't sing, hum
for what has been a wondrous life
and what is yet to come.

Tell me no forked, demonic tale
or any fearful story,
just give me leave to move, in love,
from beauty into glory.

Acceptance?

Your sane advice is logical,
it's truth one can't dispute,
but it's too pedagogical
for me to execute.

Acceptance is a fragile thing,
it wavers with the breeze;
the peace of mind it strives to bring
comes only by degrees.

So if upon some distant day
it seems that I achieve it,
and peace at last has come to stay,
I doubt if I'll believe it.

Late Bloomer

When I was in my forties,
I was so sweet and shy
I never raised my eyes to watch
the young men passing by.
　　Now I am in my fifties
　　and time is flying fast,
　　I rarely miss a single one
　　as they go strolling past.
　　　And when I'm in my sixties,
　　　if I haven't seen them all,
　　　I'll invite them by the dozens
　　　to come around to call.
　　　　　So I'll have, in my seventies,
　　　　　not one regret to bring
　　　　　to my venerable eighties,
　　　　　for I won't have missed a thing.

　　　　　And when I reach my nineties,
　　　　　if I still care,
　　　　　I'll have young men around me
　　　　　everywhere.

Facing Facts

When I recall the days of yore
when girls brought joy and jubilation
I'm sad that all there is in store
depends on my imagination.
The women who go strolling by
are looking pretty good, because
I now have problems of the eye,
and I'm not as fussy as I was.
There still are love songs to be sung
to bring enchantment to my years;
flings are still waiting to be flung —
and all I need is – volunteers.

Charity Begins

The impulse
  to give
    transcends thought.

Deeper than duty,
  more innate than intention,
    it inhabits the heart.

Where Dana dwells,
three jewels manifest
  and emptiness
   holds nothing back
    from emptiness.

Nothing is diminished
as the winds blow
and grow still.

Potential
blossoms into myriad forms,
  not to be grasped
   or hoarded.

Giving
is the spirit's wisdom
and compassion,
  refusing to accept
  the fallacy
    of giver and receiver,
     seeing only the flux and flow
      of infinity at play.

Giving And Getting

The impulse to give is instinctive.
But there's nothing like receiving.
I tried to analyze this. Here are my conclusions:
    since I have adequate food, clothing and
    accommodation, and don't enjoy vacations,
        I don't need or even desire anything else
        of a material nature.

So why do I enjoy receiving things?

It must be no more than the fact that
    it's nice to be remembered,
    to obviously have been in someone's
        spontaneous thought.

If it's expensive, so much the better,
    but I really don't care.

I may not even keep it.
Sometimes, if it has no appeal to me,
    and no earthly purpose,
    as often happens,
I hide it away and only bring it out
    when the giver is visiting.

After sufficient time has elapsed
    to ensure that the gift is forgotten,
    it may be safe to discard it or give it to
        someone else to hide.

But, all things considered, gifts are rarely a total waste.

Oh Happy Day

One breath today
draws joy
into the marrow of my bones,
   the chambers of my heart.
      I breathe one mind,
      the luminous totality,
      the consciousness that permeates each part
      of indivisible creation.
Nothing exists
except the self
in protean reality,
immanent, ineffable,
infinite manifestation.
      In every moment
      I inhale the love
      all being breathes to me
      in purest exhalation.

      I see flowers underneath my feet,
      rainbows arching overtop the street
      and haloes crowning everyone I meet.

Oh Miserable Day

First morning breath is not really the first.
It's just the earliest awareness that I exist for another day,
and confirms that once again I have survived the night.
They say the air I breathe comprises all the
     exhalations of other survivors.
Maybe that's why it doesn't always smell good.
Philosophers say that a falling tree makes no sound
     if no one hears it.
If noise is so important does it mean that
     I'm not really breathing unless I snore?
If I don't read what philosophers write
     does that erase their publications?
What a waste of thought and effort!
I am more comfortable with morbid thoughts
     than with happy ones,
because, like pessimist Schopenhauer, I expect the worst, and
like Kierkegaard and Sartre I dread having to pay for my sins.
I know that by the law of averages more things
     are likely to go wrong
     and I'm disappointed if they don't.

When I walk in the country,
I see poison ivy beneath my feet,
black clouds deciding where they'd like to meet,
and puddles on benches where I'd like a seat.

Fancy This

I go for refuge
to the primal source,
   the womb of all creation.

From the inchoate stuff
of mind,
I spin potential
into manifestation
   in conditioned, crimson threadings
   of desire
     and, winding them
     upon the shuttle
     of visualization,
I weave
a tapestry of fantasy
upon the boundless loom
of actualization.

And when the fabric crumbles into dust,
   as all eventually must,
I hail the glorious disintegration.

All comes from love,
remains as love,
returns to love.
I do not cling.
I let it go.

I take it up
and shape it, once again,
to fit my heart's unceasing jubilation.
   The grace waves
   and the particles,
   in endless undulation,
   are what I make of them.

So I will make a fabric
of gratitude and celebration,
feeding my endless appetite for joy
out of my infinite imagination.

Fancy That

I did nothing today.
What a waste!

By evening it was clear that things weren't getting any better.
No profound pondering drew forth
    some glimpse of enlightenment.
When I closed my eyes in search of ethereal imagery
        that might crystallize into some kind of awareness,
            I just fell asleep.

But my eyes felt rested.

The mystery of being eludes me. I wonder if life is
    truly supposed to have a purpose; or is it, as it appears,
        just a random occurrence.

We enjoy contacts, have conversations, make promises, break them,
    interact endlessly. But no one cares or will remember for long.
        But it helps pass the time, I guess.

Maybe tomorrow I will think of something.
    This is just an interim memo.

Think About It

What's all this fuss about mind control?
I think it's perfectly fine.
I'm a promoter of mind control,
you control yours and I'll control mine.

I've Thought About It

I have my own suggestion,
though it isn't as benign:
to settle the mind control question,
I'll control yours *and* mine.

Wish You Were There

Your presence is delightful,
but solitude is dear
and just because I miss you
doesn't mean I want you here.
I need my days to be alone,
my quiet, private place
and, even though I love you,
I don't want you face to face
for every frantic moment
of every crowded day.
So give me time and give me space
and, darling,
    stay away.

I'm Back

I can't believe this strange command
you issue so imperiously,
so I know you'll understand
if I don't take it seriously.
I easily can disappear,
it's quite a simple mission –
I have the magic words right here
I got from some magician.
I've places I can stay
when circumstances should demand it,
and I'd really stay away
      if I thought that you could stand it.

Winging It

In my dreams, I fly.
    I have flown since infancy.
I soar with hawks
and dally with butterflies.
I believe I consort with clouds.

My Freudian analyst,
assessing my damage,
is certain
that this is an escape
from repression into sexuality.

My Jungian therapist,
healing my wounds,
is positive
that this is a flight
from unacknowledged feelings
into pain-free intellect.

"Perhaps"
I concede,
unpersuaded
but mightily impressed
by expertise
and erudition.

In my heart, however,
I am convinced
that I associate with angels
and incorporeal beings
in heights of bliss
that cannot be expressed
in quotidian circumstances.
    Ecstasy often embarrasses onlookers.

So in my dreams, I fly,
not to flee reality
or to defy authority
or for any other reason
than to celebrate spirit,
    refusing to recognize
the gravity of my situation.

Dreaming

In my dreams I fall, unwillingly
    as though from an airplane,
    or off the moon's edge.

When I land it is always on my head.
    And it never hurts.

This bothers me.

I have been pondering: why this anomaly,
    this absence of pain? And I think I have the answer –
The moon must be a lot closer to the earth than I figured.

One concern haunts me.
If I ever awaken while I'm falling
I'll be in big trouble.

My analyst isn't much help.
He says he's been having the same dreams.

Well Balanced

I'm learning at last
to love myself.
Although I may stumble and fumble
I've virtues sufficient to nourish hope,
enough sins to keep me humble.

Unbalanced

I used to hate myself, feeling inadequate.
Then I observed the many foibles
of countless others.
So here's what's oddest:
I have come to recognize
      my own admirable qualities.
However, I keep this little secret to myself,
      even from my brothers,
         lest I appear immodest.

Moon Goddess

Those beloved of the moon
know that she will not be slighted;
no retiring maiden, she,
to pine for passion unrequited
but a lustrous, lofty goddess
reigning from her kingdom sky,
powerful in her commanding,
subtle sometimes, never shy.
If she chooses to espouse you,
you are well and truly mated.
She demands, for her devotion,
that it be reciprocated.
It may seem that, in the daytime,
she permits you to ignore her
but when night falls she will seek you,
find you, force you to adore her.
With a magic web of fancies
she will bind you in your sleep,
wrap you round with lambent moonbeams,
liquid fantasies that seep
to the depths of your unconscious,
blaze a longing in your mind
and your heart for her proud beauty,
let you waken then to find
you are restless, puzzled, yearning
in the silent, lonely night,
gazing skyward, lovesick, burning
for a glimpse of silver light.

My Moon Goddess

O lovely goddess of the moon,
whose beauty makes admirers swoon,
show me what ecstatic bliss is
by bestowal of your kisses.
Grant me this eternal boon,
lest, like some despondent loon,
lost without your fond caress,
I succumb and evanesce.
Elevate me like a star
to be close to where you are;
that perpetual delight
will keep your vision in my sight.
Harken to my plea, Selene,
for the powers of a genie
that you're rumoured to possess
have not always brought success.
Endymion, king in times of yore,
with whom you fifty daughters bore,
chose your tender bonds to sever
just to sleep unchanged forever,
though in the end he lost his life
for lusting after Zeus's wife.
Condescend a love to savor
that will never die or waver.
Welcome me beyond your portals,
and I'll feel like the immortals.
Then, as thou by Zeus's nod,
I, too, shall have become a god.

Sound Mind

My first teacher,
vibrant and aware,
died of cancer of the lungs.
A revered swami
succumbed to diabetes
and a venerable tulku
was borne off
by an exhausted heart.
An ancient arahat
is bent and twisted
by a painful, inexorable
progression of disease.
My meditation instructor
takes pills
for a sluggish thyroid
and a dear friend,
rich in empowerments,
is subject to
frequent bronchial infections.
A veteran
of countless retreats
wears a pacemaker
and a regular practitioner
of numerous yogas
recently experienced
emergency surgery
which has left her
with an ongoing weakness.

Knowing all this,
and acknowledging the truth
of impermanence,
I forgive the ravages that time has wrought
and absolve myself of guilt
for this unsound body.

Unsound Mind

My best friend has been
a chain smoker for 75 years
and he feels great.
His lungs are black
but he can't see them.
I said to him:
"smoking is dangerous." He replied
that he's going to stop inhaling.
But I said he'd have to stop *exhaling* too,
    because that's bad for everyone else.
Another chap I know
was sick a lot in his youth.
Then he turned 65, retired,
and began to feel great.
He says only one thing bothers him now:
    drugs are free, but he doesn't need them.
It has taken the fun out of being well.
My cousin has been on diets all her life.
She goes up ten pounds,
    loses them, up fifteen, then the same thing.
She still weighs the same today, but over the years
she has lost 368 pounds altogether.
My mother-in-law got a prescription
for pills to lose weight.
After a few months without results she complained.
    The doctor asked: "Did you take one
    before each meal, as I told you?"
Answer: "No, just after meals."
"Why didn't you follow my orders?"
"When I took them before meals they killed my appetite."

A sound body may last longer.
but apparently it isn't worth it.

Every Little Bit

You don't have to be perfect to help.
It's a long, narrow road to perfection,
but the good that you do on the way will insure
that you move in the proper direction.
Don't fret about the doing it right,
if it's mastery that you're pursuing,
just open your heart and then go ahead, start.
The practice improves with the doing.
The skill and the wisdom will come.
You'll learn from the teachers who've found
they need us beginners and unpolished sinners;
there aren't enough saints to go round.

No Do-Gooder

I'd like to respond to your plea,
but doing what's right isn't me.
I hate to decry it,
some day I may try it
and that would be something to see.
Though there's pleasure in being a winner,
I'm happier being a sinner,
so give me some scotch
and a chance to debauch,
and then I'll be ready for dinner.
Remember, dear sisters and brothers,
most good is accomplished by others,
so preserve me from promise or fetter;
when you're perfect, who wants to be better?

That's All There Is

It's too late to be loved for my body,
it's too crass to be loved for my cash,
and I'm not so naïve
that I'd ever believe
you could go for my style and panache.
To be loved for my mind would be witless,
my intellect's not where it's at.
Which leaves, on the whole,
my immaculate soul.
Do you think you could love me for that?

Anything's Possible

The immaculate soul is a fiction,
that's an obvious, provable fact.
But your body is not,
and if it can be bought,
I'll endeavour to do it with tact.
Your appearance is very appealing,
and I think I can live with your mind,
so I hope you'll agree
to accompany me,
and together we'll prove love is blind.

Reflection

Eternity's hard to imagine;
I'm doing the best that I can
to conceive of the never-ending void
before the beginning began.
Infinity's even harder
and guaranteed to confound;
it's just too vast for me to grasp
or wrap my mind around
But my heart understands the scope of love,
limitless and eternal,
so I just sit and love the love
and jot it in my journal.

More Reflection

I've read of travel, time and space
and how they intertwine,
learned space and time may be reversed
(the theory isn't mine);
and I desired to try it once,
to see if it was wrong,
but changed my mind upon deciding
it would take too long;
my spaceship might run out of gas,
or weaken at the seams,
so I await the final truth
to greet me in my dreams.

News Commentary

We don't understand the minds of our children,
I doubt that we ever will.
We raise them on violence, blood and aggression
and then we're surprised when they kill.

We don't understand the mind of the universe.
Look at the lives we live,
full of hatred and greed and the stubborn refusal
to see that we get what we give.

We don't understand how to be fully human,
to reach out and join hand to hand
and deliver ourselves to that great revelation
which, so far, we don't understand.

Commentary On Children

When children are starting to grow and to learn,
beset with sensations wherever they turn,
they change with a subtlety hard to discern
in response to the countless impressions.

If we train them with kindness, love and respect,
avoiding indifference, fear and neglect,
those children will probably choose to select
behaviour devoid of transgressions.

When children grow up as a group of aberrants
they're merely exhibiting traits of inherence
that move them to mimic the acts of their parents,
with often unwholesome obsessions.

The remedy only can come from within,
if integrity, honesty, decency win
over bigotry, fear, and a penchant for sin …
it may take psychiatrical sessions.

Bitching, Moaning, Whines and Grumbles

The bricks spall, the mortar crumbles.
The knees shake, the hand fumbles,
the mind slips, the tongue stumbles,
the gut growls, the tummy rumbles.
Jack falls and Jill tumbles.
Growing old sure humbles.

Me Too

Don't gripe or feel blue;
I'm falling apart too.
Can't hear and don't see,
drink lots but can't pee,
memory slips as capacity dips,
and, like most old-timers,
pursued by Alzheimer's.

Poem For Today

Even last month,
if you had turned up at my door
I could have cast the past away
for only that and nothing more.
I would have recklessly ignored
experience's warnings and alarms
for the remembered joy of coming home
to the small circle of your arms.
A month ago,
hope might have washed away the fears
that spread their isolating residue
over my years
and I, perhaps, (oh surely)
would have stepped out of the husks
of pain and pride
into the still communion I once felt
at simply being by your side.
Only last month,
if you had come, by chance,
and found me waiting in the wings
and beckoned me,
I might have dared to dance.
And just your presence
would have spoken all you had to say,
    last month,
        last week,
            yesterday.

I Miss You Too

At least a hundred times or more
I started dialling your phone,
dreading those lonely days in store
since I've begun to dwell alone.
Yet I retain a stubborn streak,
I guess you've known it for a while,
so, since I hate appearing weak,
apologizing's not my style.
It's possible that I was wrong,
(I'm hoping that this sounds sincere)
but that's not happened for so long
it's not a likelihood I fear.
But I'll admit the truth to you,
which brings your virtues to the fore,
it's so hard finding someone new
it's you I must be looking for.
Last month, last week and yesterday
thoughts of you ever came my way,
so let the bygones be gone by;
I've missed you more than "now and then."
Let's give ourselves another try
and if that fails, we'll try again.

Catharsis

When it started to bother me greatly
and I couldn't contain it sedately,
I shouted my anger to seven black crows.
Wherever they carried it, only God knows,
but I haven't seen much of it lately.

Revenge

Well, I'm not very happy to learn it,
and I know I did nothing to earn it,
but those crows, filled with glee,
dumped the problem on me,
so I'm glad to know where to return it.

Depth Recollection

In my heart
I watched a bed of tender shoots
pierce through the soil
and, in an instant, rise
to leaf and bud and glorious flower.

And I awoke
with joy for beauty recognized so swift in its arising,
with sorrow for beauty realized so sudden in its passing.

And, as I held the dream,
there sprung, from my own matrix, memory
that every bloom is rooted in totality
and, though it withers, droops and disappears,
returns its essence to the universal source,
it bears back to the womb of all creation
the sustenance of the bliss of being.

All of experience is mingled at the font;
no blossom springs in isolation
but is confluent in its depth
with the bright, fundamental nature
of all that is made manifest.

Nothing is ever lost.
Death nurtures life
and, in the heart of each brief burst of glory,
I see the face of one I loved.

Superficial Reflection

A volcano erupts
    and spews from earth's bowels
    a new island made of nothing but cooled lava.

Time elapses, and plants begin to grow.
Then animals arrive, as though from space,
    like a creation by a super-magician,
    the reaction to an action.

Similarly, each word we hear,
    every object we observe,
    each experience we endure
    leaves a permanent imprint on our psyches,
    making us basically different persons,
    affecting our future actions and decisions.

Therefore we might be expected to become continually wiser
    and freer from failings and inadequacies.

But this doesn't often happen.

Thus I must conclude
    that it is sometimes possible that the total
    can be less than the sum of all its parts.

Long Range Romance

I have learned, in my dotage,
whatever befall
I must love from a distance
or not love at all.

Better by furlongs
a trifle aloof,
a tittle afar
than under one roof.

Vastly preferred,
as everyone knows,
to coming to grips
or coming to blows.

Not caught in the grasp
or caught in the act,
mileage maintains
illusion intact.

Passion is all
very well, in its place,
but give me an interval,
give me some space.

When next you're in town,
come by for a night
of amorous ecstasy,
bliss and delight,

of the damp spot that always
ends up underneath
my quivering haunches,
of hair in my teeth,

of a kitchen reduced
to a cluttered condition
and a toilet seat left
in the upright position.

Then leave in the morning,
while ardour still rages,
and go someplace where
I won't see you for ages.

I'll love you much longer,
I'll love you much better
by e-mail or telephone,
postcard or letter.

I'll probably love you
all of my life
if you visit but rarely
and live with your wife.

Short Range Romance

I have learned from experience
love that is dear
is better enjoyed
when the lover is near.

You cannot deny
that in foul or fair weather
it's twice as much fun
when we're sleeping together.

What harmony when
you conform to your mold,
and are happy to do
everything that you're told.

Long distance problems
are likely to worsen,
but I can solve anything
if it's in person.

Absence, for some,
makes the heart become fonder;
for me it's a signal
to stray and to wander.

Whenever you feel
that my company smothers,
just give me a call
and I'll look for some others.

So when you decide
I should just be a friend,
don't keep it a secret
but call it, the end.

Remember, with me
there's an absence of danger
which can't be assumed
when you're out with a stranger.

But if my proximity
brings you content,
I'll promise you things
and keep paying the rent.

We'll revel in joys
unconfined and delirious.
My wife doesn't mind
'cause she knows it's not serious.

Polishing My Footwork

Recognizing the oneness,
the unity of being,
I shall harbour no ill will.

I will have no enemies,
not disgruntled relatives
or disappointed suitors
or drivers who cut me off in traffic.
Not dog owners who don't scoop
or cyclists who terrorize the sidewalks
or politicians who exempt themselves from precepts.
Not surly waiters
or apathetic sales clerks
or well-meaning but misguided gentlemen
who bring to crowded elevators
the reek of a magnum of aftershave.
Not the incompetent, the indifferent, the inane.

I will cultivate compassion
to temper my righteous indignation,
acknowledging my participation
in even the clumsiest steps
of the dance.

Imperfection

When people exasperate me
    I know I should respond with
     understanding and forgiveness, but rarely
    do they engender this courtesy in me.

I do not let myself get into a rage
    or become filled with hatred, because
    I know that wouldn't be good for me.
    But I do get indignant and annoyed.

Waiters nod pleasantly while ignoring my request
    for "well done" or "hot soup."
    Once it took three tries but the soup was still
    lukewarm.
    They were teaching me a lesson, I guess,
    as though *I* were the slow learner.

I can forgive injury, but never – cold soup.

My intolerance for
    the most blatant failings of others
    is not blunted by an acute awareness
    of my own imperfections.

However, I try to forgive them,
    mainly because I can't figure out
    how to get even.

Poem Egg

I can but offer it a nest
and keep it safe and warm.
It hatches, in its own good time,
its own peculiar form.

Poem Aborted

Sometimes my poem can exist
aloft beside some wayward mist
until, in vagrant currents caught,
it vanishes, in search of thought.

Infinity Is Not A Big Number

I count my blessings
    – more than I would ever
     have believed
and realize
    I leave a
    countless number more
unacknowledged,
     not, as yet, perceived.

Breaking Even

I count my virtues,
    numbering almost to infinity,
    if you count minor ones,
    generally overlooked.
This leaves me little time
    to enumerate my failings,
    which may reach a similar total,
    if the figures aren't cooked.

The Play's The Thing

I always assume
that the mike is open,
that someone's listening,
that I'm going on live,
that this whole great drama
is a public performance
and my parents and my relatives
are coming down the drive.

There's nothing that's private,
everything's connected,
hooked up and communicating.
That's the simple fact.
And whatever I am thinking,
saying, doing,
is shared with the family.
So I'm polishing my act.

Plot For A Play

I write a play of ancient lore,
dramatis personae are four.
Each one a soul in torment bares.
It doesn't matter, no one cares.

It's opening night, the stage is lit,
each star when summoned enters it,
endeavoring, for his future's sake,
to keep the audience awake.

They stride, gesticulate and bellow
in the manner of Othello;
all are equally effective
in delivering invective.

Dramatic last scene, big mistake,
real bullets used instead of fake,
the error such that none can mask it,
so each one exits in a casket.

The net result is not so bad;
even the audience isn't sad.
The backers almost do a war dance:
the deal just called for one performance.

Yes I Am

I take refuge in the moment,
always in the moment.
The when and then are worrisome
and burdensome to me.
What was and what could be
distract me from what is
and what is
is all there is
(or ever was or will be)
as far as I can see.
The power and the glory
are present in the present
and I'm pretty much exactly
where I want to be.

No I'm Not

I'm seldom thinking of today,
although I know I should.
It's strange that I became this way;
I know it isn't good.
But memories of yesterday
invade my waking moments,
or else it's dreams of things to come
that are today's opponents.
It's clear to me that all we have
is rooted in the present,
but day-dreams are my magic salve
that makes today so pleasant.

Sense Of Purpose

What can I offer to totality,
  the source of all made manifest?
What can I give in gratitude
  for this extraordinary life

Only to act as mirror to the all,
  reflecting self to self,
    another facet
      on the infinite jewel of creation.

Look, I say,
I give you the uniqueness of experience
of this infinitesimal cell
of your eternal being.

Here is the smell of roses
to this particular nose
and this is the stench of diesel fumes.
This is the slide of silk along this skin,
the touch of fingertip to lip.
Here is how the breath feels,
breathing in,
trickling, flowing, rushing out.
This is the act of chewing, tasting,
  bitter, salty, sour and sweet.
And this is walking,
watching how the feet
are lifting, moving, placing,
on concrete, carpet, grass.

This is the celebration of the intellect,
the joyous leap of intuition.
Here is the issue of your root
growing to limitless fruition.
This is the swirl of love,
the rush of fear,
the body's fireworks serpent of
sensation.

This is devotion.
This is adoration.

The full awareness of the senses
and of mind
I strive to offer you in every moment,
to feed into the universal consciousness
this aspect, this view,
this yet another flavour of perception,
this blissful expression of participation,
   like a child's drawing
    to be hung on God's refrigerator door.

Looking For A Connection

Once I sent a drawing for God to hang on his refrigerator door.
It came back with a note that said He was out of magnets.

I don't say He lied. Maybe He was just not impressed with it, or
perhaps He was too busy.

It's even possible, I guess, that He really had run out of them.

I don't remember offending Him, but lately He has been
ignoring my calls.
He never used to. So I figured:

> what if the problem is that God needs an assistant?
> I would like that job. You know, the way doctors let nurses
> handle the less dramatic cases.
>
> There could be voice mail, or the call could be rerouted to me
> directly: "This is Joe at 1-800-GOD-HELP. What's the problem?"

Most likely I would have to refer some cases back to the Boss.
Better that than have my decisions overridden. I'm very
sensitive about that sort of thing.

I admire Linda's absorbing reflections and benevolent philosophy.
But I can't be as full of enthusiasm and optimism, because
I think God has made a lot of mistakes.

There have been times when I felt like giving Him advice.
But I'm glad I didn't.

Time Out

We were always One.
There was only One;
there never was
anyone else.

But just to make the sport more scary
we played at the game of adversary
and hid ourselves in mysteries
swathed in our separate histories
and dreamed of finding One.

But it was always One.
One hung upon the cross,
One sat beneath the bodhi tree
and One was good
and One was bad
and One was all there'll ever be,
  shaman and cynic, sinner and saint.

Behind the mask,
beneath the paint,
beyond the blade of arbitrary time,
there has been One,
  integral and sublime
being whatever, however, whoever it chose to be,
  being you,
  being me,
  being itself in myriad manifestation.

And, not to spoil the game,
but just to have a moment's celebration,
let's recollect with love and jubilation
that we are One.

Oneness and Twoness

I was always two:
the person manifest, available to scrutiny,
and the hidden me,
with secret thoughts and fanciful dreams;
not Janus-faced
for purpose of deception,
but with two faces
waiting for selection,
one focused on
the doorway called "beginning,"
the other on
the portal labelled "ending,"
with both enjoined
against the thought of sinning,
and bent on solving
problems that are pending:

or maybe just trying to see
both sides of the question
in an effort to be impartial,
or else to render a more logical decision
not subject to some subsequent derision.

    But Linda,
seeing you fathom, as you have,
the oneness of creation,
inherent in the concept of oblation,
eliciting your feeling of elation,
convinces me
that your genes should be offered
    to science
    for multiple cloning,

because you're of such sterling stuff
    that one of you is not enough.

Singularity

I am shrinking,
  not becoming shy,
  like a shrinking violet,
    but becoming shorter,
    dwindling in stature.
I was never formidable
but now I border on petite,
heading toward insignificant.
I look up more often
and frequently stand on my toes.

I am not particularly concerned;
size is of no great importance to me
unless it affects the fit of my clothes.
I do not feel compelled to measure up.

But I speculate and extrapolate.

Will I diminish
into the desiccated dregs
of an abandoned vessel,
to ride like sibylline dust
on the winds of eternity?

Or will the good things increase
as the package gets smaller,
growing more dense
till I collapse on myself
like a spent star,
drawing creation into me,
spinning light and matter
on my event horizon,
confounding space and time,
  as well as friends and family,
becoming my own tunnel
to another universe?

Enlarging

I am expanding.
not like some growing corporation.
More like a balloon full of hot air.
Not conceited, but somewhat impressed.
In my normal size nobody notices me.
I can't wait until I can be recognized for my merit.
Talent eludes me. But I have virtues,
even if I am the only one aware of them.
So I inhale helium and shun carbon dioxide.
I don't mind buying new clothes for the new inflated me
but whenever possible I get "one size fits all," just in case.

Then I wonder:
at what pressure will I explode, revealing the awful truth of my
    insubstantiality.
Or is my skin so elastic that I can become a new star
    or maybe a moon?
At which time, will astronauts try to land on me?
Will they be too heavy?
If I am a moon, will earthlings be able to see me smile?
If they colonize me, will I end up as polluted as Earth?

I worry about such things.

Maybe I should just stay the way I am.
Get rid of the gas, regardless of consequences.

If I am determined to become well known,
I can simply advertise.

Geriatric Valentine

When the pheromones have weakened
and the chemistry is odd,
will we still be held together
though the bonds are frayed and flawed?

With the drying of the juices
and the damping of the lust,
do you think we could be left with
an emotion we can trust?

When estrogen's exhausted
and testosterone has dwindled
will we still have more in common
than a spark that can't be kindled?

When our passions have been tempered
and our gonads have been tamed,
can we warm each other's cockles
without getting all inflamed?

If our pleasure centres petrify
when dopamine deprived,
will we find our hearts still tender?
Will affection have survived

or will we be separated
by a wide, abysmal chasm
when we concede that there is
no potential for orgasm?

I'd be very disappointed,
I'd be terribly distressed
if we found we have no mutual attraction
when we're dressed.

My Geriatric Valentine

Should weariness beset me,
if I fail to go the distance,
I can manage, if you let me,
with mechanical assistance.

Should orgasmic sessions thrill you
and become a constant need,
I'll endeavour to fulfill you –
but it wouldn't hurt to plead.

If the help you need is great,
and it seems you cannot do it,
if you're free to stay up late
maybe I can talk you through it.

When I cannot, on demand,
and your need is even greater,
I'll be glad to lend a hand,
or provide you with a satyr.

The reason making love to you
may seem inept or skewed
is that it takes a day or two
to get me in the mood.

I always try to please you,
don't call me a fuddy-duddy,
for I'll do much more than tease you –
if you let me bring a buddy.

If I don't achieve success
and all my promises seem lies,
should you end up feeling stress
and anger, I'll apologize.

For Jaredene

Who can I tell about you?
You were the one I told everything to
and even before I could say it, you knew.
Now who can I tell about you?

Friends don't come easy to me.
I know lots of people, but those I feel free
to confide in and open my heart to are few.
So who can I tell about you?

You never did the usual thing.
You opened my eyes and you managed to bring
to every occasion a fresh point of view.
I never could tell about you.

Everything changes and passes away,
sometimes even love is no reason to stay.
We all have to do what we all have to do.
But who can I tell about you?

We shared our joy and we shared our pain
in a symbiosis I can't explain.
Just like Christopher Robin and Pooh,
we made a oneness out of two
and I don't know how. And I don't know who
I can possibly tell about you.

The Spirit Replies

I am keenly aware of your wants,
and I wish you could hear my response;
if you could you'd be able to see
there is no need to tell about me.

For you ought to admit what is true,
I was just as beholden to you,
and those memories sparkling and glistening
I earned just by being there, listening.

And the intimacy that we shared
just reflected the way that we cared,
with our speech a revolving of doors,
and my thoughts just a mirror of yours.

So whenever you wish to confide,
and there's no confidant by your side,
just pretend I had not gone away,
and I'm sure you could guess what I'd say.

And it might just console you to know
that my spirit continues to grow,
while my memory, vibrant and true,
keeps me constantly thinking of you.

Song Of The Frigid Woman
or
Baby, It's Cold Inside

Oh Lord, please give me an impotent man.
I enjoy a good hug whenever I can
but celibacy is my ultimate plan,
so, give me an impotent man.

He could be taking some strong medication
that dampens his drive, or have some combination
of injury, age, ennui and castration,
just give me an impotent man.

I haven't completely abandoned romance,
I just choose to relate where there isn't the chance
stepping out might involve stepping out of my pants.
Please give me an impotent man.

No thrill in the masculine member I find
since my worn out libido just up and resigned,
but I love intercourse with the masculine mind,
so give me an impotent man.

The truth must be told and the facts must be faced,
no man in his prime or his senses would waste
a moment in chasing the forcibly chaste,
so give me an impotent man.

Oh Lord, please don't send me some lusty young buck
because I'm convinced, with my usual luck,
I'd want conversation and he'd want to
    physically express his affection.
Oh, give me an impotent man.

The Impotent Man

If the story you tell is really true,
I am the perfect man for you.
If you truly are a platonic seeker,
you'll never find a man who's weaker.

And though there are times when I perform,
it's quite a departure from the norm.
If capacity comes, and I employ it,
I promise I will not enjoy it.

My ardor was once beyond compare,
but now you will find I just don't care.
So when you find me in your bed,
it's just to discuss the books I've read.

And though this may not be sensational,
you might find it educational.
If it will help secure me preference,
I can supply you with one reference.

Should something occur that's not conventional,
just assume it was unintentional.
If someone comes to please you more,
I'll be no worse off than before.

And finally, since I feel inventive,
how is this for an incentive –
if our relationship should end,
I'd recommend you to a friend.

LINDA M. STITT

My mother read poetry to me when I was in her womb and I emerged, I am told, in Huntsville, Ontario, crying in iambic pentameter. With the encouragement of my parents, I was composing verses as soon as I could talk.

I was educated in Georgetown and Toronto and lived for many years in Thunder Bay, where I began the process of what Carl Sagan described as "matter coming to consciousness."

The exploration continues even now that I have exceeded my shelf life and surpassed my best before date.

In view of the fact that my work has been known,
on occasion, to rhyme,
I consider myself an anachronism
    in my own time.

JOE FROMSTEIN

I was born in Toronto and graduated as a pharmacist in 1940.
World War II was raging, so a month after graduation I enlisted
in the Royal Canadian Air Force. This brought me a guided
tour of Europe lasting five and a half years, during which I was
never consulted about the itinerary.

After running my own pharmacy from 1950 to 1984 I retired
and returned to the University of Toronto to take a Bachelor of
Arts course. The main subjects were English Literature,
Linguistics, and Creative Writing. I got my B.A. the year I
turned eighty. During my studies I wrote some plays, short
stories, and a series of humorous poems based on characters
from Greek Mythology.

Two years ago I joined Toastmasters International, an
organization which guides people in communicating and public
speaking. I had fun writing and performing speeches and even
won a few "humorous speech" contests. Since then I've been
enjoying being physically and intellectually active, playing
tennis, working out and writing poems in an effort to stave off
the inevitable. So far it has worked pretty well.

Over the years the buffeting whims of fate have brought
work, marriage, children, widowhood, and other adventures.
Meanwhile I keep writing, focusing on the light side of things,
even when the results disguise within them a kernel of truth or
introspection.

The following poems are reprinted with the kind permission of
their author Linda Stitt and her publishers.

Artichokes
Late Bloomer
Conformity
Poem Egg

Adjust Your Set copyright ©1997 by Linda Stitt,
published by Natural Heritage / Natural History Inc.

Song Of The Frigid Woman, Or Baby, It's Cold Inside
Poem For Today
Cold Comfort

Uncritical Mass in Consort copyright ©1995 by Linda Stitt,
published by Sadhana Press

The First Time
For Jaredene

Bliss Pig copyright ©1999 by Linda Stitt,
published by Natural Heritage/Natural History Inc.

How Was It For You, Baby?
Long Range Romance
Charity Begins
Sense Of Purpose
Depth Recollection
Time Out
Polishing My Footwork

Passionate Intensity copyright ©2003 by Linda Stitt,
published by Seraphim Editions

Falling Flat
Geriatric Valentine
Oh Happy Day
Singularity

LOVEPLAY

ORDER FORM

If you enjoyed reading these wonderful poems and
want to share them with family or friends,
order a copy of LOVEPLAY today.

Please rush me _____ copies of **LOVEPLAY** at
$16.95 CDN/$12.95 US each.

(GST, shipping and handling included)

Enclosed is a cheque or money order made payable to
White Knight Publications in the amount of :

$_____

Please mail my book(s) to:

Name: _____

Address: _____

_____

Province: _____ Postal Code: _____

Telephone #:_____

E-mail address (optional): _____

To received your book(s), mail your cheque or money order to:
White Knight Publications
Suite 103, One Benvenuto Place
Toronto, Ontario M4V 2L1 Canada

PLEASE ALLOW THREE TO FOUR WEEKS FOR DELIVERY
OR
FOR MORE INFORMATION OR TO ORDER FROM OUR WEB SITE:
www.loveplaybook.com

What is **LOVEPLAY** all about?

LOVEPLAY is a *tour de force* wordplay of two scintillating minds whose humour, wisdom and warmth will cheer and comfort those who have love, those who want love and those who don't give a hang about love…but still delight in seeing others suffer.

ABLAZE with luminous words and lucid awareness **LOVEPLAY** rejuvenates rhyme and reinvigorates romance in sophisticated tales of love and seduction.

LIFT YOUR SPIRITS with this joyous heart-felt work and be surprised by its intimate revelations.

MORE COMMENTS ABOUT LOVEPLAY

Mike Bullard, stand-up comic/ talk-show host: "At eighty-five years old, Joe Fromstein possesses the wisdom of a much older man."

Vince Calandra Sr., Talent Executive, *Ed Sullivan Show:* "Wonderful book! I thoroughly enjoyed it. The poems are humorous and poignant at the same time. A rare find."

Don Beck, Executive Producer, *Eight Simple Rules, Two Guys and a Girl*: "Why couldn't the poetry I studied in school have been more like this?"